Conceptions of the Universe

How our conceptions of reality arise from the limitations of our perceptual apparatus

John King

123 Books

Copyright © 2011 by John King

All rights reserved. This book, or parts thereof, may not be reproduced in any form without permission.

A catalogue record for this book is available from the British Library

ISBN: 978-1-907962-26-4

Published by 123 Books

Reading, England

For David

Contents

Preface 7

Introduction 11

1 Conception and Perception 15

2 Is one's perceptual apparatus inevitably constrained? 34

3 Various views concerning how similar one is to one's surroundings 49

4 Conclusions 92

Preface

We ordinarily take the universe to be as it appears to us to be. So, when one observes a red rose in one's garden, one ordinarily assumes that the part of the universe that is one's garden contains a red rose.

However, when one takes oneself outside of one's ordinary state of interaction with the universe; when one starts to reflect and rationalise about the nature of one's relationship with the universe; then, things become more complicated than the state of affairs belied by our 'ordinary' assumptions.

When one reflects it becomes clear that for every perceiver there is a *different* world. The world that appears to a typical human is different to that which appears to a typical cat, and these worlds are different to the world that appears to a typical bat. Furthermore, many humans are not 'typical' – many humans perceive a different world to the majority of humans. There also 'untypical' cats and bats.

Why is this so? It is simply because the world that appears to a perceiver partially results from the perceptual apparatus of the perceiver. Every perceiver plays a part in creating the world that appears to them. Obviously, if two perceivers have identical sets of perceptual apparatus, and Perceiver A was to be swapped for Perceiver B, then Perceiver B would perceive exactly the same things that Perceiver A perceived. It is when sets of perceptual apparatus have significant differences that 'different' worlds are created. To be clear, every world is a unique creation but some of these unique creations can be 'different' and some can be 'non-different'.

With this in mind, let us consider how our conceptions of reality arise from the limitations of our perceptual apparatus.

Introduction

This book is ultimately concerned with what humans can know about the nature of the universe. The starting point of our investigation into the nature of the universe is to consider the issue of how one conceives of oneself in relation to one's surroundings. One's surroundings – assuming that there is a world surrounding one – clearly have a particular degree of similarity to one. That is to say, one has a particular range of attributes *and* one's surroundings have a particular range of attributes. However, there is a plethora of ways in which one could conceive of one's surroundings in relation to one.

Conceptions of the universe

That is to say, one's surroundings have a particular bundle of attributes – Bundle S* – but there are a plethora of different conceptions which one could possibly have concerning which bundle of attributes one's surroundings has – Bundle A*, Bundle B*, Bundle C*, Bundle Z*, etc. At the extremes one could conceive of one's surroundings as exceptionally similar to one or as exceptionally dissimilar to one. In other words, one could conceive of one's surroundings as having the vast majority (or all) of the attributes that one has *or* one could conceive of one's surroundings as having barely any of the attributes that one has.

Introduction

Why is the fact that one could conceive of one's surroundings very differently important? It is important because it means that there will be a plethora of different views concerning the nature of the universe. In *Chapter One* I consider the relationship between one's conception of one's surroundings and one's perception of those surroundings. In *Chapter Two* I consider whether the way in which one gains information about one's surroundings is inevitably constrained by one's perceptual apparatus. These chapters set the scene for *Chapter Three* in which I consider various views concerning how similar one *actually* is to one's surroundings. Finally, in *Chapter Four,* I draw some conclusions.

Chapter 1

Conception and perception

Let us start by considering the conception one has of one's surroundings. This conception is grounded in perceptions of those surroundings. If one did not have perceptions of one's surroundings then one could not have any meaningful conception of those surroundings; conception without perception would be mere speculation (if one has no perceptions of anything outside of one then one will have no knowledge about anything outside of one).

Conceptions of the universe

One perceives one's surroundings in a number of different ways; however, for a typical human it is visual perception which plays the central role in forging a conception of their surroundings. One's visual perception typically presents one with a forever changing view of the world; this view contains both things which appear to be static and things which are clearly moving. The things which are clearly moving move in a diverse array of patterns. For example, I perceive a bird flying through the sky, branches of trees bristling in the wind, cars moving along roads, humans walking on pavements, clouds gliding through the sky, leaves falling from a tree, and hands moving around on a clock face. In contrast to these moving things I also

Conception and perception

perceive things which are currently apparently static such as a dining table and chairs, a carpet, a sofa, some books on a shelf, and a cup on a table. It is these perceptions of apparently static things and diversely moving things which underpins how one conceives of one's surroundings.

Let us consider a particular movement which is perceived in one's surroundings. It is possible that this movement could be conceived in a number of different ways. How is this possible? It is possible because one's beliefs can cause one to conceive of one and the same movement differently. So, one's conception of one's surroundings arises when one's (largely visual) perceptions of those surroundings

Conceptions of the universe

are filtered through a particular belief system concerning those surroundings. A belief system is simply a set of mutually supporting beliefs. In any era a number of different belief systems concerning the nature of human surroundings are likely to exist. In the world today there are a variety of such systems instantiated in different humans.

In a particular epoch it is likely that one belief system will be dominant; that is to say, it is likely that a particular belief system will be instantiated in the majority of living humans. It is, of course, also likely, if not inevitable, that a dominant belief system will ultimately be dethroned by an alternative system.

Conception and perception

In order to explore the relationship between one's perception of one's surroundings and one's conception of one's surroundings I will focus on two particular human belief systems – the Primal World View and the Modern World View. It is widely accepted that in the past the Primal World View was the dominant human belief system *and* that the Modern World View replaced the Primal World View as the dominant human belief system. Richard Tarnas describes the Primal World View as follows:

> The primal human perceives the surrounding world as permeated with meaning...Spirits are seen in the forest, presences are felt in the wind and the ocean, the river, the moun-

tain...The primal world is ensouled. It communicates and has purposes. It is pregnant with signs and symbols, implications and intentions. The world is animated by the same psychologically resonant realities that human beings experience within themselves...Creative and responsive intelligence, spirit and soul, meaning and purpose are everywhere.[1]

In the Primal World View one's perceptions of one's surroundings are filtered through a belief system in which all of those surroundings are conceived of as very similar to one. The Modern

---

[1] Richard Tarnas, *Cosmos and Psyche*, Plume, USA, 2007, p. 16.

Conception and perception

World View which supplanted the Primal World View as the dominant worldview which is described by Tarnas as follows:

> The modern mind experiences a fundamental division between a subjective human self and an objective external world...Whatever beauty and value that human beings may perceive in the universe, that universe is in itself mere matter in motion, mechanistic and purposeless, ruled by chance and necessity...The world outside the human being lacks conscious intelligence, it lacks interi-

ority, and it lacks intrinsic meaning and purpose.[2]

In this belief system one's perceptions of one's surroundings are clearly filtered through a belief system in which the overwhelming majority of one's surroundings are conceived of as very different to one; there is a "fundamental division" between humans and their surroundings – humans are subjective and non-mechanistic, whilst human surroundings are objective and mechanistic (there is scope *within* the Modern World View to include some non-human animals on the human side of the "division"). These two world views – the Primal

---

[2] Richard Tarnas, *Cosmos and Psyche*, Plume, USA, 2007, p. 17.

Conception and perception

World View and the Modern World View – are not just sets of detached beliefs; they are different ways of being in the world. It should be noted that whilst the Modern World View supplanted the Primal World View as the dominant worldview the Primal World View still exists, and the fact that a particular belief system has supplanted a rival system for dominance obviously does not entail that the supplanting system is the best guide to the actual nature of human surroundings.

Let us consider these two different belief systems – the Modern World View and the Primal World View. It seems fairly uncontroversial to assume that if one went *far enough* back into human

Conceptions of the universe

history that of the two belief systems only the Primal World View would have existed. If this is so it means that at some later time the Modern World View first arose as a belief system, and then at a still later time this belief system was sufficiently pervasive to become the dominant human belief system. The question is: What caused the emergence and the increasing pervasiveness of the Modern World View? In other words, why did the majority of humans come to conceive of their surroundings as fundamentally different to themselves?

The most plausible answer seems to be the fact that throughout human history humans have increasingly developed the ability to master their

Conception and perception

surroundings – to shape them to serve their needs. This increasing mastery was clearly dependent on detailed observations of the *movements* that humans perceived in their surroundings. Through noting regularities in these movements, and by thinking about these regularities, humans increasingly became able to predict future movements in their surroundings. Initially this increasing predictive ability was located *within* the Primal World View. However, when this predictive ability passed a certain threshold this catalysed a reconceptualisation of the surroundings; in this reconceptualisation the *overwhelming majority* of movements in one's surroundings are envisioned as predictable and mechanistic – mere matter in motion. In this way

Conceptions of the universe

the Modern World View was born. At some stage – possibly thousands of years after its inception – the Modern World View supplanted the Primal World View as the dominant world view.

So, when a human who has the belief system of the Modern World View perceives hands moving around on a clock face, or leaves falling from a tree, they believe that these movements are *in principle* predictable. They take *themselves* to be able to predict the future movements of the hands around a clock face: "they will continue to move at the same speed and in a clockwise direction". If this prediction turns out to be false – the hands actually change in speed and/or direction – then the explanation moves to science: *"if I had full scientific knowledge* about the state of the clock and its immediate surroundings then I would have been able to predict that the hands would actually start speeding up and moving in an anti-clockwise direction". This "full scientific knowledge" belief applies to leaves falling from a tree – one might not believe that one can actually predict the exact movements of the leaves, but one believes that if one had full scientific knowledge that one would be able to predict these movements.

The beliefs outlined in the previous paragraph are *implicit beliefs* instantiated in humans who are part of the Modern World View. So, the increasing ability to *predict* movements caused the vast majority of movements to be conceived of as *mechanistic*, and the mechanistic conception then caused the belief that these movements are, in principle, *predictable by science*. The same scientific level explanation is assumed to exist for the overwhelming majority of the movements in one's surroundings. In other words, the Modern World View involves the implicit belief that humans are *in principle* able to predict the overwhelming majority of the movements in their surroundings irrespective of whether or not one is actually able to predict them.

Conception and perception

Let us consider how the human who has the belief system of the Modern World View conceives of the movements in their surroundings that are other humans. Are the movements of these humans also conceived of as movements which are predictable either by oneself or in principle by science? Of course, there are those who do conceive of other humans in this way. They believe that a completed science would enable one to predict all of the movements of other humans, and would enable their own movements to be predicted by others. However, this belief system is clearly not the Modern World View. For, as we have seen, according to the Modern World View humans (and possibly some non-human animals) are unique. In the Modern World View

Conceptions of the universe

whilst the overwhelming majority of the movements in one's surroundings are conceived of as mechanistic / *in principle* predictable, the movements of humans are conceived of as non-mechanistic / *in principle* unpredictable. In other words, there is conceived to be a radical difference in kind between the movement of a raindrop falling through the atmosphere and the movement of a human falling through the atmosphere. Of course, some human movements are predictable, but this misses the point; one can conceive of something as *in principle* unpredictable and still be able to make some successful predictions concerning that thing.

Conception and perception

What supports this disjointed view of the world? It is surely the belief that one has freedom how to move, and that if one has this freedom one's movements must, in principle, be unpredictable / non-mechanistic. It follows that if one views oneself in this way that one will view other humans in this way; it would be most odd to believe that oneself had freedom and thus moved in ways which are *in principle* unpredictable, but that the movements of other humans were *in principle* predictable – mere matter in motion. In contrast, as we have seen, the vast majority of movements are conceived of as mechanistic *because* of the human ability to predict these movements.

Conceptions of the universe

Let us conclude. The links between one's perceptions of one's surroundings and one's conception of one's surroundings have been explored through considering how the Modern World View came to supplant the Primal World View. It is clear that humans who share the same perceptual apparatus can have very different conceptions of their perceived surroundings. According to the Primal World View there is no fundamental division in the world. According to the Modern World View there is such a division – the world is conceived as being divided into a mechanistic part in which movements are *in principle* predictable, and a non-mechanistic part in which movements are *in principle* unpredictable.

Conception and perception

Of course, these are just two belief systems among many. Some new worldviews have recently been emerging which are centred on quantum physics. According to many of these views – as with the Primal World View – there is no fundamental division in the world. So, it is possible that in the future the *dominant* human belief system will be one in which the fundamental division inherent in the Modern World View has been eliminated; in such a view either *all* of the movements in the world will be considered to be *in principle* predictable / mechanistic, or *none* of the movements in the world will be considered to be *in principle* predictable / mechanistic.

Chapter 2

Is one's perceptual apparatus inevitably constrained?

In the previous chapter we saw that the conception one has of one's surroundings is grounded in one's perceptions of those surroundings. It follows that if the way in which one gains information about one's surroundings is inevitably constrained by one's perceptual apparatus that one's conception of one's surroundings is highly likely to be misguided or incomplete. If such an inevitable perceptual con-

One's perceptual apparatus

straint exists there would be varying degrees of 'conceptual mistakenness' as the realisation that one's perceptions are inevitably constrained could cause one to change one's belief system. Of course, it is possible that this change could result in one having a less accurate conception of one's surroundings. However, it is perhaps more likely that the change would lead to the adoption of one of a range of possible belief systems which more accurately matches the actual nature of one's surroundings. In other words, the human who realises that their perceptual apparatus is inevitably constrained is likely to have a more accurate conception of their surroundings than the human who denies the existence of the inevitable constraint.

Conceptions of the universe

This outcome is likely because, as we will see, the inevitable constraint causes one to *conceive* of one's surroundings as dissimilar to one, and it is likely – given an evolutionary view of one's surroundings – that *in reality* one is actually quite similar to one's surroundings. So, does such an inevitable constraint exist? And could there actually be a number of different inevitable constraints?

In order to answer these questions it is useful to distinguish a 'constraint' from an 'inevitable constraint'. There are few who would deny that the way in which one gains information about one's surroundings is constrained by one's perceptual apparatus. After all, it is well known that other

One's perceptual apparatus

animals, such as dogs, can hear sounds that the human perceptual apparatus is unable to perceive. This means that there is information in one's surroundings which one is unable to perceive because of the structure of one's perceptual apparatus. Is this constraint an inevitable constraint? One could reasonably argue that this type of constraint is not an inevitable one because it is theoretically possible that a technological implant into a human ear could cause that human to hear exactly the same range of sounds as a dog. Even if this were possible the case should alert us to the likelihood that one's surroundings contain vastly more information than one's perceptual apparatus is typically able to perceive.

Conceptions of the universe

The question before us is if the human perceptual apparatus is *inevitably* constrained. There are different ways in which the apparatus could be so constrained. One way in which there would be an inevitable constraint would be if there was information in one's surroundings which one's perceptual apparatus was *in principle* unable to perceive. No amount of technological modification would enable one to perceive such information. Is there such inaccessible information? A seemingly good candidate for such information is states of raw feeling such as the pain of other humans. One might be able to perceive that a human is almost certainly suffering from excruciating pain from the sights and sounds one perceives but this is a very different thing from being able to perceive the *feeling* of the pain itself. It seems obviously true that states of raw feeling like this are *in principle* imperceptible to one's perceptual apparatus. They are states of one's surroundings which exist (presuming that other humans exist and contain states such as the feeling of pain) but which one is unable to perceive because of the inevitable constraints of one's perceptual apparatus.

Another way in which the human perceptual apparatus would be inevitably constrained would be if its operation entailed an inevitable moulding of its surroundings; this 'moulding' constraint would be an inevitable constraint on *all* perceptual apparatus and so could not be technologically overcome. If this constraint exists then one would not have access to what one's surroundings were like when they were in an 'unmoulded' state. In its most extreme transcendental idealism form this moulding would entail that one inevitably perceives a world in space and time but that the unmoulded world is aspatial and atemporal. A slightly less extreme version of this perceptual moulding is argued for by those who hold that perception collapses quantum wavefunctions. On this view the unperceived world contains spatio-temporal wavefunctions which collapse into a particular form when perceived. If this were so, then one would, of course, have no access to the world in its unperceived state. A more widely held version of

One's perceptual apparatus

the 'moulding constraint' is advocated by those who claim that the unperceived world is spatially extended but wholly devoid of secondary qualities such as colour. On this view one's surroundings are actually wholly devoid of colours when they are unperceived – it being the 'perceptual moulding' of those surroundings which makes it appear as though they are coloured. It is, of course, possible both that when one's surroundings are unperceived that they are coloured *and* that the colours one perceives are dependent on the 'moulding' of one's perceptual apparatus. All of the possibilities discussed in this paragraph lead to the conclusion that one's perceptual apparatus is inevitably constrained.

Conceptions of the universe

There is one more way in which the human perceptual apparatus seems to be inevitably constrained. It seems obvious that the human perceptual apparatus has in-built temporal constraints. Specifically, the human perceptual apparatus is only able to perceive movements from an exceptionally narrow temporal perspective. This is perhaps a hard thing to envision. How is one to get a handle on this inevitable constraint? A starting point is perhaps to take an evolutionary perspective. One could reasonably argue that the human perceptual apparatus has evolved to perceive the kind of movements that are of survival interest. These would clearly be short-term movements because humans are animals with a short-term lifespan. One needs to

One's perceptual apparatus

be able to perceive short-term movements such as the running of a wild animal towards one if one is to survive. It should be remembered that the most reasonable thing to believe is that one's surroundings have been evolving and moving in various ways for billions of years; but, in contrast, the average contemporary human will be very lucky to reach the age of one hundred years. One can barely comprehend what it would be like to perceive a movement pattern that spanned a thousand years or a million years; but such movements clearly exist.

How exactly does the exceptionally narrow temporal perspective from which humans are able to perceive movements constrain one's perceptions? It

Conceptions of the universe

is perhaps helpful to start by considering a relatively short-term movement which one could, *in principle*, be able to perceive. So, there is no reason why one could not perceive the movement pattern that is the Earth taking 365 days to move around the Sun. If one was located in an appropriately positioned space station, and was able to stay in a continuous state of perception for 365 days, then one would be able to perceive this movement (of course nearly-all, if not all, humans alive at the moment would not be able to do this as they need to sleep!). Of course, if we start to consider slightly longer-term movement patterns, those that exceed one's lifespan, then it is obviously the case that it is impossible for one to be able to perceive these movement patterns (one can only perceive whilst one is alive!).

Why is this important? Quite simply, if one only has perceptual access to a small temporal slice of a movement pattern, then one is not in a position to judge whether that movement is *in principle* predictable/mechanistic or *in principle* unpredictable/non-mechanistic. Let us consider a series of very short-term movements such as all the movements of the players on the pitch in a 90 minute football match. If one perceived this series of movements one would, no doubt, conclude that they were unpredictable/non-mechanistic. However, if one only had perceptual access to the first millisecond of the match what would one conclude? The movements which one perceived within this temporal window would surely not appear to one as unpredictable/non-mechanistic. It is only if one has a longer time slice of perceptual data that one is able to see that the movement one previously perceived is part of a movement pattern which one would now wish to assert is fundamentally unpredictable/non-mechanistic.

So, when a human perceives a particular movement and conceives of this movement as mechanistic this conception could be wrong due to the inevitably temporally constrained way in which the human perceptual apparatus operates.

One's perceptual apparatus

We have seen that the way in which one gains information about one's surroundings is inevitably constrained; the open question is the extent of this constraint. It is likely that the inevitably constrained way in which one gains information about one's surroundings will cause one to conceive of those surroundings as more dissimilar to one than they actually are. However, if one realises that one's perceptual apparatus is inevitably constrained then one is able to adopt a new belief system; a system which attempts to offset the effect of one or more of the inevitable constraints. Given the nature of the constraints we have explored it is likely that the recognition of their existence will cause one to

Conceptions of the universe

conceive of one's surroundings as more similar to one.

So, given that some people do not acknowledge that the human perceptual apparatus is inevitably constrained, *and* that there are a number of different ways in which one can adjust one's belief system in an attempt to compensate for one or more of the inevitable constraints, it is not surprising that there are a variety of views concerning how similar one is to one's surroundings.

Chapter 3

Various views concerning how similar one is to one's surroundings

The considerations from the previous two chapters put us in a good position to understand why there are a variety of views concerning how similar one is to one's surroundings. In *Chapter One* we saw that different views of similarity can arise when the perceptions of one's surroundings are filtered through different belief systems. We encountered two fairly extreme belief systems – the Primal World

View and the Modern World View. In *Chapter Two* we saw that different views of similarity can also emerge when one recognises that one's perceptual apparatus is inevitably constrained; the recognition itself being the basis for the formation of new belief systems as one seeks to offset the effect of one or more of the inevitable constraints.

Let us now consider a number of different contemporary belief systems.

3.1   Physicalism

A widespread contemporary view of human surroundings (and humans themselves) is 'physicalism' – also known as 'materialism'. This view is typically closely associated with the Modern World View. This typical association is perhaps surprising, for physicalism is the view that *everything* that exists is physical; given this one might think that the physicalist would conceive of their surroundings as very similar to them, rather than as radically different to them.

The curious association between physicalism and the Modern World View raises the following question: What does it mean for a thing to be physical? According to the *theory-based conception*: "A property is physical if and only if it either is the sort of property that physical theory tells us about or else is a property which metaphysically (or logically) supervenes on the sort of property that physical theory tells us about"[3]. According to the *object-based conception*: "A property is physical if and only if it either is the sort of property required by a complete account of the intrinsic nature of paradigmatic physical objects and their constituents or else is a property which metaphysically (or logically) supervenes on the sort of property required by a complete account of the intrinsic nature of paradigmatic physical objects and their constituents"[4].

---

[3] Stoljar, Daniel, "Physicalism", **The Stanford Encyclopedia of Philosophy (Fall 2009 Edition)**, Edward N. Zalta (ed.), URL = <http://plato.stanford.edu/archives/fall2009/entries/physicalism/>.

[4] Stoljar, Daniel, "Physicalism", **The Stanford Encyclopedia of Philosophy (Fall 2009 Edition)**, Edward N. Zalta (ed.), URL = <http://plato.stanford.edu/archives/fall2009/entries/physicalism/>.

Various views of similarity

The *theory-based conception* of the physical faces an obvious problem. For, according to Hempel's dilemma, this conception leads to physicalism either being trivially true or false. If physicalism is defined in terms of contemporary (incomplete) physics it will be false. However, if physicalism is defined in terms of a completed physics then it is trivial as nobody knows which properties would be present in a completed physics.

For this reason the *object-based conception* of the physical is the more plausible option. On this view a property is physical if a complete account of paradigmatic physical objects includes that property. Such a complete account clearly exists in theory, the question is: Can a complete account of paradigmatic physical objects be known by a human? If one realises that the way in which one gains information about one's surroundings is inevitably constrained by one's perceptual apparatus then one will have a very compelling reason to doubt that such a complete account can be attained. This realisation is clear in the following assertions from Immanuel Kant, Peter Unger, Bertrand Russell, and Galen Strawson:

> For every substance, including even a simple element of matter, must after all have some kind of inner activity as the ground of its producing an external effect, and that in spite of

the fact that I cannot specify in what that inner activity consists...Leibniz said that this inner ground of all its external relations and their changes was a power of representation. This thought, which was not developed by Leibniz, was greeted with laughter by later philosophers. They would, however, have been better advised to have first considered the question whether a substance, such as a simple part of matter, would be possible in the complete absence of any inner state.[5]

---

[5] Immanuel Kant, "Dreams of a Spirit-Seer", in *Theoretical Philosophy 1755-1770*, ed. David Walford, (New York: Cambridge University Press, 1992), p. 315.

Conceptions of the universe

> Except for what little of the physical world we might apprehend in conscious experience, which is available if Materialism should be true, *the physical is mysterious to us.*[6]

> we know nothing about the intrinsic quality of physical events except when these are mental events that we directly experience.[7]

> I take physicalism to be the view that every real, concrete phenomenon in the universe is ... physical...I will equate 'concrete' with 'spatio-temporally (or at least temporally)

---

[6] Peter Unger, *All the Power in the World*, Oxford, Oxford University Press, 2006, p. 5.

[7] Bertrand Russell, *Portraits from Memory*, Spokesman, 1956, p. 153.

Various views of similarity

located', and I will use 'phenomenon' as a completely general word for any sort of existent. Plainly all mental goings on are concrete phenomena... But how can experiential phenomena be physical phenomena? Many take this claim to be profoundly problematic (this is the 'mind-body problem'). This is usually because they think they know a lot about the nature of the physical. They take the idea that the experiential is physical to be profoundly problematic *given what we know about the nature of the physical*. But they have already made a large and fatal mistake. This is because we have no good reason to think that we know anything about the physical that gives us any reason to find any problem in the idea that experiential phenomena are physical phenomena.[8]

Once one has realised – like these philosophers have – that one's perceptions of one's surroundings are inevitably constrained there are various paths one can take. One option is to assert that physicalism is true, that a complete account of the world will only include physical properties; it is just that there are physical properties which one is perceptually barred from. However, this acceptance of unknown physical properties clearly opens the floodgates to a

---

[8] Galen Strawson, *Consciousness and its place in nature,* Imprint Academic, Exeter, 2006, pp. 3-4.

number of varieties of physicalism. One could advocate 'emergent physicalism', 'panwhat-it-is-likeness physicalism', or 'panawareness physicalism'.

It is perhaps debatable whether some of these positions should be thought of as varieties *of* physicalism, or as *non-physicalist monisms*. The other option open to one is to reject monism and to advocate dualism. Let us consider these various possibilities.

Conceptions of the universe

3.2 Emergent Physicalism

It is possible to accept that the entire universe is wholly comprised of physical objects, and that paradigmatic physical objects such as trees and tables have physical properties which one is perceptually barred from knowing anything about, but also to maintain that these unknown physical properties are wholly devoid of 'what-it-is-likeness'. That is to say, it is possible to believe that they are wholly devoid of feeling states such as pain, tingling and 'pins and needles'.

On this view humans are physical objects, and humans clearly have 'what-it-is-likeness', so some physical objects do have 'what-it-is-likeness'. This

Various views of similarity

view – that the physical is mostly devoid of 'what-it-is-likeness' and that it is only in certain parts of the physical that 'what-it-is-likeness' emerges – I am referring to as 'emergent physicalism'. On this view 'what-it-is-likeness' emerges.

Emergent physicalism seems to be intuitively plausible as one ordinarily does not suppose that a table contains 'what-it-is-likeness'. However, the emergent physicalist needs to give an account of the coherence of such a disjointed world view. How is it possible that physical stuff which itself is wholly devoid of 'what-it-is-likeness' when it is arranged in a certain way can generate 'what-it-is-likeness' when it is arranged in a slightly different way? Such emergence is not beyond the realms of possibility, but giving a convincing account of the intelligibility of such emergence is deeply problematic; indeed, some philosophers go so far as to argue that such emergence is incoherent. For example, Galen Strawson argues that:

> Does this conception of emergence make sense? I think that it is very, very hard to understand what it is supposed to involve. I think that it is incoherent, in fact, and that this general way of talking of emergence has acquired an air of plausibility (or at least possibility) for some simply because it has been

Various views of similarity

appealed to many times in the face of a seeming mystery.[9]

It is, of course, common for certain properties to emerge with complexity; this is unproblematic. The question is about the intelligibility of the notion of 'what-it-is-likeness' properties emerging out of arrangements of stuff that are wholly devoid of 'what-it-is-likeness'. Strawson claims that:

> liquidity is a truly emergent property of certain groups of H_2O molecules. It is not there at the bottom of things, and then it is there... But can we hope to understand the

---

[9] Strawson, Galen, *Consciousness and its Place in Nature*, Imprint Academic, Exeter, 2006, p. 12.

alleged emergence of experiential phenomena from non-experiential phenomena by reference to such models? I don't think so. The emergent character of liquidity relative to its non-liquid constituents does indeed seem shiningly easy to grasp...But when we return to the case of experience, and look for an analogy of the right size of momentousness, as it were, it seems that we can't make do with things like liquidity, where we move within a completely conceptually homogenous (non-heterogeneous) set of notions. We need an analogy on a wholly different scale if we are to get any imaginative grip on the supposed move from the non-experiential to the experiential.[10]

Strawson claims that an analogy of an appropriate scale would be the emergence of the extended out of an arrangement of the wholly unextended, and asserts that this "should be rejected as absurd".[11] Of course, if this is an analogy of the appropriate scale then the emergence of 'what-it-is-likeness' does seem to be absurd; the question is whether it is an analogy of the appropriate scale. Catherine Wilson asserts that: "it is hard to see why it is

---

[10] Strawson, Galen, *Consciousness and its Place in Nature*, Imprint Academic, Exeter, 2006, pp. 13-15.

[11] Strawson, Galen, *Consciousness and its Place in Nature*, Imprint Academic, Exeter, 2006, p. 15.

Conceptions of the universe

impossible that what one needs for there to be experiences in the universe is a brain made of insentient molecules put together in a certain way"[12]. Of course, one should agree with Wilson that one should not assert that the emergence of 'what-it-is-likeness' out of that which is wholly devoid of 'what-it-is-likeness' is impossible. The real issue seems to be not impossibility but likelihood. It is clearly possible that the physical is pervaded by 'what-it-is-likeness', and it also clearly possible that 'what-it-is-likeness' exists in only parts of the physical.

---

[12] Wilson, Catherine, "Commentary on Galen Strawson", in Strawson, Galen, *Consciousness and its Place in Nature*, Imprint Academic, Exeter, 2006, p. 182.

Various views of similarity

However, the idea that 'what-it-is-likeness' can emerge out of that which is wholly devoid of 'what-it-is-likeness' is clearly a contentious one. All that the supporter of such emergence can do is just assert that they have faith that it happens; accounts of emergence such as liquidity are clearly not going to convince those who think that the emergence of 'what-it-is-likeness' is incoherent.

Given that the idea that 'what-it-is-likeness' emerges is deeply problematic the question of why the emergent physicalist believes that such emergence occurs needs to be addressed. In other words, the question is: Why does the emergent physicalist *deny* that all of the physical has 'what-it-is-likeness'?

Conceptions of the universe

The main motivation for this denial simply seems to be that oneself is the only thing that one indubitably knows has 'what-it-is-likeness', and it is this knowledge which causes one to suppose that parts of one's surroundings which resemble one also have 'what-it-is-likeness' – parts such as other humans and some non-human animals. In contrast, a table and a tree seem to be most unlike one, so why should one suppose that such things contain 'what-it-is-likeness'?

The problem with this line of reasoning by analogy is, of course, that one's perceptions of one's surroundings are inevitably constrained by one's perceptual apparatus; if one's perceptions were not

Various views of similarity

so constrained then one might conclude that the entirety of one's surroundings resembled one, and hence that all of one's surroundings contained 'what-it-is-likeness'.

There are several variants of emergent physicalism each of which attempts to account for why only certain parts of the physical have 'what-it-is-likeness'. One position is reductive physicalism; according to this view some physical states *are* states of 'what-it-is-likeness' but most physical states are not. Another position is non-reductive physicalism; according to this view states of 'what-it-is-likeness' arise when particular arrangements of physical states exist, but they are not reducible to these states, and most arrangements of physical states do not give rise to 'what-it-is-likeness'. Another position is functionalism according to which arrangements of physical states with particular functional roles involve 'what-it-is-likeness'; of course, according to this version of emergent physicalism the vast majority of function performing arrangements of physical states do not involve 'what-it-is-likeness'.

So, the emergent physicalist defends the view that only *some* parts of the physical have 'what-it-is-likeness'. This is in contrast to the eliminativist who (quite bizarrely) holds that 'what-it-is-likeness' does not exist, and to both the panwhat-it-is-likeness

Various views of similarity

physicalist and the panawareness physicalist, for whom 'what-it-is-likeness' pervades *all* of the physical.

3.3 Panwhat-it-is-likeness Physicalism

According to this view one's surroundings are wholly comprised of physical objects, and paradigmatic physical objects such as trees and tables have physical properties which one is perceptually barred from knowing anything about. We have seen that the emergent physicalist can also accept these two assertions. However, in contrast to the emergent physicalist the panwhat-it-is-likeness physicalist believes that these unknown physical properties are 'what-it-is-likeness' properties. The motivation for this view is that the central problem which the emergent physicalist faces – giving an intelligible account of the emergence of 'what-it-is-likeness' – is dissolved as, on this view, the physical is pervaded by 'what-it-is-likeness'.

The explanation given of where the emergent physicalist has gone wrong is that the emergent physicalist has founded their view of emergence based on the perceptions of their inevitably constrained perceptual apparatus; if they fully realized the nature and extent of this limitation they could overcome the problem they have created by extend-

Various views of similarity

ing 'what-it-is-likeness' from *some* of the physical to *all* of the physical.

What exactly does it mean to assert that all of the physical is pervaded by 'what-it-is-likeness'? What it means in a broad sense is that every part of the physical contains qualitative feeling. It is worth pointing out that to say that the physical is pervaded by 'what-it-is-likeness' is *not* to say that the physical is pervaded by 'mind' *or* that it is pervaded by 'awareness'. In denying that awareness pervades the physical the panwhat-it-is-likeness physicalist clearly needs to give an intelligible account of the emergence of awareness out of the wholly unaware.

Conceptions of the universe

3.4 Panawareness Physicalism

According to this view one's surroundings are wholly comprised of physical objects, and paradigmatic physical objects such as trees and tables have physical properties which one is perceptually barred from knowing anything about. We have seen that both the emergent physicalist and the panwhat-it-is-likeness physicalist can also accept these two assertions. In contrast to these two views the panawareness physicalist believes that these unknown physical properties are awareness properties.

Is it possible to believe that the physical is pervaded by awareness but *not* by 'what-it-is-likeness'? This is a possibility which shouldn't be discounted outright because it is intelligible that a state of awareness could exist in the absence of 'what-it-is-likeness'. However, in practice it is hard to envision anyone advocating this position, as whilst it solves the problem of how it is possible that awareness could evolve out of a world that is wholly devoid of awareness, the deeper problem of how 'what-it-is-likeness' could evolve out of a world that is wholly devoid of 'what-it-is-likeness' would remain unresolved. This means that, in reality, those who advocate panawareness physicalism believe that all states of 'what-it-is-likeness' are states of awareness.

Conceptions of the universe

So, the panwhat-it-is-likeness physicalist is able to evade the problem faced by the emergent physicalist of having to give an intelligible account of how a certain arrangement of physical states can be wholly devoid of 'what-it-is-likeness' whilst a slightly different arrangement can give rise to 'what-it-is-likeness'. The panwhat-it-is-likeness physicalist is able to evade this problem *without* believing that all of the physical is aware. Whilst, the panawareness physicalist also evades the problem faced by the emergent physicalist, but is led to the conclusion that all of the physical is pervaded with awareness.

Philosophers who are panawareness physicalists are typically referred to either as panpsychists or panexperientialists. However, there appears to be no difference between these two positions as both the panpsychist and the panexperientialist are united in their belief that 'what-it-is-likeness' (i.e. 'experience') is a mental or psychical phenomenon, that this phenomenon entails awareness, and that this phenomenon pervades the physical world. This is clear in the following two assertions from panexperientialist David Ray Griffin, the first of which attempts to justify his invention of the term 'panexperientialism':

> "Panpsychism" is the term that has generally been used for this position. "Panexperientialism" is preferable, however, for two reasons:

Conceptions of the universe

(1) The term "psyche" suggests that the basic units endure through long stretches of time, whereas they may be momentary experiences; and (2) "psyche" inevitably suggests a higher form of experience than would be appropriate for the most elementary units of nature.[13]

experience always involves some minimal awareness of *what is* [14]

---

[13] David Ray Griffin, *Unsnarling the World- Knot*, Wipf and Stock, Eugene, 2007, p. 78.

[14] David Ray Griffin, *Unsnarling the World- Knot*, Wipf and Stock, Eugene, 2007, p. 130-31.

Various views of similarity

Perhaps Griffin's use of the term 'panexperientialism' rather than 'panpsychism' is partly motivated by the over-the-top reactions that some have to the word panpsychism. For example, McGinn claims that: "[Panpsychism] is metaphysically and scientifically outrageous."[15] Perhaps the hope is that McGinn would not consider panexperientialism to be quite so outrageous. However, the point is that panexperientialism is not a different position from panpsychism as panpsychists also agree with Griffin's two assertions above, that: (1) the basic units may be momentary experiences and (2) the basic units have a lower form of experience

---

[15] McGinn, Colin, *The Character of Mind*, (Oxford: Oxford University Press, 1982), p. 32.

than certain more complex arrangements of such units. This is clear in the following quotes from panpsychist advocates Galen Strawson, David Bohm and Ervin Laszlo:

> we will have to wonder how macroexperientiality arises from microexperientiality, where by microexperientiality I mean the experientiality of particles relative to which all evolved experientiality is macroexperientiality.[16]

---

[16] Strawson, Galen, *Consciousness and its Place in Nature*, Imprint Academic, Exeter, 2006, p. 26.

Various views of similarity

in some sense, a rudimentary mind-like quality is present even at the level of particle physics.[17]

psyche is [not] present throughout reality in the same way, at the same level of development. We [panpsychists] say that psyche evolves, the same as matter.[18]

The idea that there are different levels of experience within the physical is a crucial element in panpsychist/panexperientialist views. It is this

---

[17] Bohm, David, "A new theory of the relationship of mind and matter", *Journal of Philosophical Psychology,* 3 No.2, 1990, p. 283.

[18] Laszlo, Ervin, *Science and the Akashic Field*, (Vermont, Inner Traditions, 2004), p. 147.

conception which gives rise to the 'combination problem'. William Seager describes this problem as follows: "explaining how the myriad elements of 'atomic consciousness' can be combined into a new, complex and rich consciousness such as that we possess."[19] Put slightly differently, it is the problem of how to give an intelligible account of how 'micro' experiences sum to form a 'macro' experience. Formulating such an account is no easy task. William James argued that such 'combination' is logically untenable:

---

[19] Seager, William, "Consciousness, Information and Panpsychism", *Journal of Consciousness Studies*, 2 No.3, 1995, p. 280.

Various views of similarity

Take a hundred of them [feelings], shuffle them and pack them as close together as you can (whatever that might mean); still each remains the same feeling it always was, shut in its own skin, windowless, ignorant of what the other feelings are and mean. There would be a hundred-and-first feeling there, if, when a group or series of such feelings were set up, a consciousness *belonging to the group as such* should emerge. And this 101st feeling would be a totally new fact; the 100 feelings might, by a curious physical law, be a signal for its *creation*, when they came together; but they would have no substantial identity with it, nor it with them, and one could never deduce the one from the others, or (in any intelligible sense) say that they *evolved* it. [20]

Despite believing that such combination is logically untenable James ultimately concluded that it must somehow occur. Similarly, in considering the varieties of physicalism Strawson claims that "some sort of panpsychism must be true"[21] but admits that he has no account of combination; indeed, Strawson "enthusiastically agree[s]"[22] with Philip Goff's

---

[20] James, William, *The Principles of Psychology - Volume 1*, (New York: Dover Publications Inc., 1950), p. 160.

[21] Strawson, Galen, "Realistic Monism" in Ed. Skrbina, David, *Mind that Abides*, (Philadelphia: John Benjamins Publishing Co., 2009), p. 64

[22] Strawson, Galen, "Realistic Monism" in Ed. Skrbina, David, *Mind that Abides*, (Philadelphia: John Benjamins Publishing Co., 2009), p. 64.

Various views of similarity

assertion that Strawson simply has "faith that it must happen somehow".[23]

In short, the panawareness physicalists James and Strawson believe that combination must occur but they cannot explain how it could possibly occur. In contrast, it is possible that the panwhat-it-is-likeness physicalist has the tools to be able to give an intelligible solution to the 'combination problem'.

3.5   *Dualism*

In response to the realisation that one's perceptions of one's surroundings are inevitably constrained one

---

[23] Goff, Philip, "Experiences Don't Sum", in Strawson, Galen, *Consciousness and its Place in Nature*, Imprint Academic, Exeter, 2006, p. 26.

Conceptions of the universe

option is to reject all of the physicalist monisms outlined above and to advocate dualism. That is to say, one could assert that some of one's surroundings are physical and some are non-physical. However, once it has been acknowledged that the nature of the physical is barred from one – that one does not know what the physical is – then it is far from clear what it means to talk of the non-physical. This means that, in reality, all of the physicalist positions outlined in the previous three sections can be repackaged and relabelled as 'dualist' positions.

So, rather than being an 'emergent physicalist' one could be an 'emergent dualist' and claim that the 'what-it-is-likeness' properties which emerge in parts of one's surroundings are 'dualistic' rather than 'physicalistic' properties. In this vein the 'dualist' Richard Swinburne claims that:

> the fact of evolution is evident. Even more evident, to my mind, is the fact that what has evolved is different, radically and qualitatively, from that from which it has evolved. Rocks and rivers are not conscious; they do not have thoughts, sensations and purposes; but men, and some animals, do have thoughts, sensations, and purposes.[24]

---

[24] Swinburne, Richard, *The Evolution of the Soul*, p. 1.

Conceptions of the universe

On this view the evolved 'dualist properties' are of a "radically" different nature to 'physical properties' but this belief is hard to defend if one is forced to admit that one doesn't know the nature of 'physical properties'. Whichever property one isolates and asserts is an evolved 'dualist property' could actually be a 'physical property'.

So, when one asserts that a paradigmatic physical object such as a table is wholly devoid of sensations, that sensations are actually a 'dualist' property which emerge in "some animals" then one is mistakenly claiming to know the nature of the physical, to know that the physical is wholly devoid of sensations.

Various views of similarity

Another possibility for the dualist is to agree with the 'panwhat-it-is-likeness physicalist' that all of the physical is pervaded with 'what-it-is-likeness', and that awareness is something which only emerges in parts of one's surroundings. The 'panwhat-it-is-likeness dualist' can then disagree with the 'panwhat-it-is-likeness physicalist' about the nature of awareness; whilst the 'panwhat-it-is-likeness physicalist' claims that awareness is physical, the 'panwhat-it-is-likeness dualist' claims that it is non-physical.

The third possibility for the dualist is a modified version of 'panawareness physicalism'. On this account the 'panawareness dualist' asserts that a

Conceptions of the universe

human contains a 'physical' part which is wholly devoid of awareness and 'what-it-is-likeness', and also contains a 'non-physical' part which contains awareness/'what-it-is-likeness'. This applies not just to humans, for according to the 'panawareness dualist' *all* of one's surroundings contain both of these substances too.

Our consideration of how the three physicalist monisms can be repackaged as dualist positions seems to lead us to the conclusion that once one acknowledges the inevitably constrained way in which one gains information about one's surroundings that there is no intelligible difference between those who claim to be 'physicalists' and those who claim to be 'dualists'. These two positions only exist in opposition to each other because of the failure to acknowledge the inevitable constraint. It is this failure which can lead one to erroneously conclude that they know the nature of the 'physical'.

Chapter 4

Conclusions

We have seen that we ordinarily take the universe to be as it appears to us to be – when one perceives a red rose in one's garden one ordinarily assumes that the part of the universe that is one's garden contains a red rose.

However, we have seen that one's perceptions can be conceptualised in many different ways (as in the Primal World View versus the Modern World View). Furthermore, we have seen that one's perceptions are inevitably constrained, which means

Conclusions

that the conceptualisations that one makes of one's perceptions are not accurate conceptualisations of the universe – they are merely conceptualisations of one's constrained perceptions.

This means that there are many diverse views as to how similar one is to the rest of the universe. Those who do not acknowledge the existence of the inevitable constraints are more likely to believe that they are dissimilar to the rest of the universe. Whilst, those who realise that the inevitable constraints exist have a good reason to believe that the universe is quite similar to them.

In terms of the various positions we have explored the panwhat-it-is-likeness physicalist and

Conceptions of the universe

the panawareness physicalist are more likely to acknowledge the existence of the inevitable constraints; indeed, such acknowledgement might be the reason for adopting that particular view in the first place.

What is likely to happen if one accepts that the conceptions one has of the universe arise from the limitations of one's perceptual apparatus? That is to say, what is likely to happen if one realises that the universe itself is likely to be very different to one's conceptions?

Well, if one believes that the universe is an evolving entity that slowly changes through time, and that everything that now exists has evolved from

Conclusions

the singularity of the Big Bang, then one might have a good reason to change one's view of the universe. If the universe is a slowly evolving interconnected whole then there is a good reason to believe that the attributes of humans are also likely to be pervasive attributes in the universe. In other words, there is a good reason to believe that the non-human universe might be far more similar to the human universe than we ordinarily take it to be.

To put this another way, we have a good reason to reject Emergent Physicalism and to embrace either Panwhat-it-is-likeness Physicalism or Panawareness Physicalism. Emergent Physicalism seems to be the position that most closely approximates the way that we ordinarily take the universe to be, but it is a disjointed view of the universe. According to this view humans are very dissimilar to the majority of the universe. We have seen that this view has a seemingly intractable problem at its core – attempting to make sense of the emergence of what-it-is-likeness out of that which is wholly devoid of what-it-is-likeness.

Once the inevitable perceptual constraints are acknowledged this problem can be overcome because one can accept that there is no good reason to believe that any part of the universe is wholly devoid of what-it-is-likeness. One can accept that the universe is fundamentally similar throughout.

Other books by the author:

What is Creativity? : Originality, Art & Invention
(2011)

www.ingramcontent.com/pod-product-compliance
Lightning Source LLC
Chambersburg PA
CBHW071310040426
42444CB00009B/1957